A VISUAL JOURNEY THROUGH

SPACES &
STRUCTURES

by M. Soledad Girolami

NTRY-WAY

how entryways set the tone for the rest of the home
nspiring collection of images. From grand foyers to cozy
xplore diverse styles and creative ideas that transform
en-overlooked spaces into welcoming portals. Whether
eking to make a bold statement or create a subtle, stylish
ion, this section offers a range of designs to spark your
ion and elevate your entryway.

CURVES & *CURVES*

Curves are making a bold comeback in contemporary interior design, adding a touch of sophistication and warmth to spaces. Gone are the days of rigid, straight lines dominating every room. Today's designs celebrate the beauty of fluid, organic shapes that soften the edges of modern spaces. Curved furniture, rounded architectural details, and flowing forms not only enhance aesthetic appeal but also create a more inviting and comfortable environment. Embrace the trend of curves to infuse your home with a sense of graceful movement and timeless elegance.

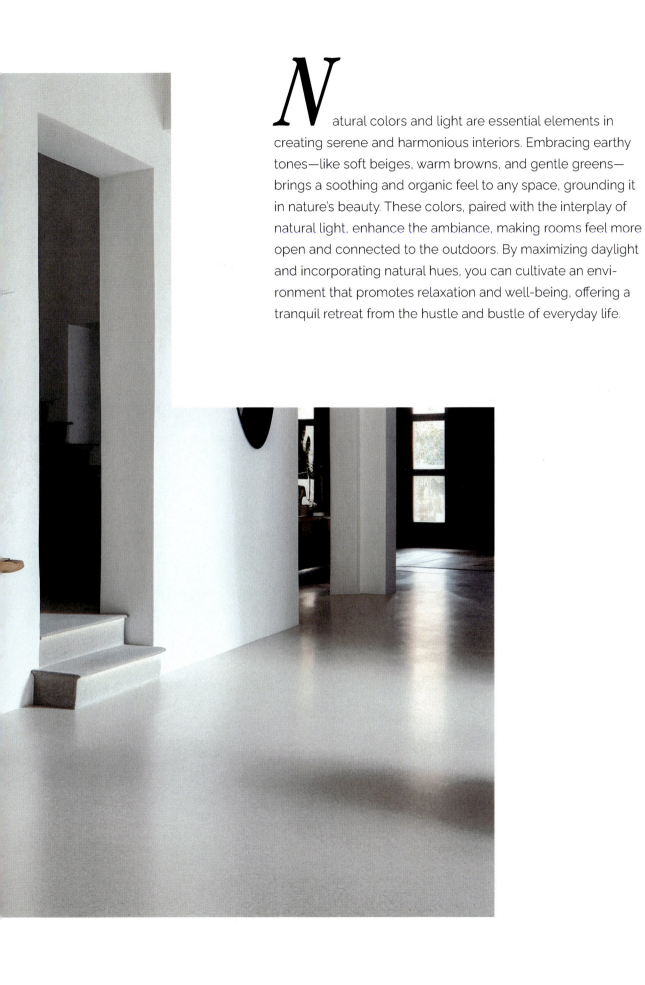

*N*atural colors and light are essential elements in creating serene and harmonious interiors. Embracing earthy tones—like soft beiges, warm browns, and gentle greens—brings a soothing and organic feel to any space, grounding it in nature's beauty. These colors, paired with the interplay of natural light, enhance the ambiance, making rooms feel more open and connected to the outdoors. By maximizing daylight and incorporating natural hues, you can cultivate an environment that promotes relaxation and well-being, offering a tranquil retreat from the hustle and bustle of everyday life.

TIMELESS
WOOD

Wood remains a quintessential material in interior design, celebrated for its versatility and enduring charm. Whether used in structural elements like beams and columns or crafted into elegant furniture, wood adds warmth, texture, and a touch of nature to any space. Its natural grains and hues create visual interest and a sense of authenticity, while its durability ensures long-lasting beauty and functionality. From modern minimalism to classic rustic styles, wood's adaptability allows it to seamlessly integrate into various design aesthetics, making it an essential choice for creating both functional and visually stunning interiors.

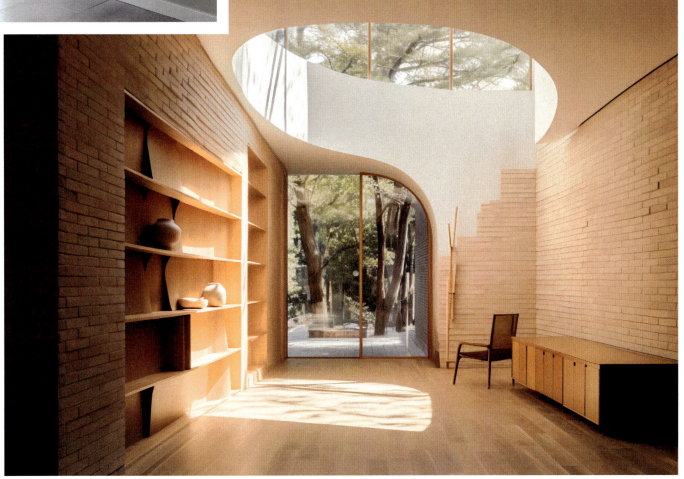

MOODY STYLE

Moody spaces are all about creating environments that evoke a sense of depth, intrigue, and emotional resonance. By embracing rich, dark tones, layered textures, and dramatic lighting, these spaces offer a sanctuary from the everyday. The interplay of shadows and subdued hues can transform a room into a cozy retreat or a sophisticated haven, encouraging relaxation and contemplation. Whether through the use of deep blues, lush greens, or earthy browns, and complemented by strategically placed lighting, moody interiors bring a unique intensity and character to your home, making every space feel profoundly personal and inviting.

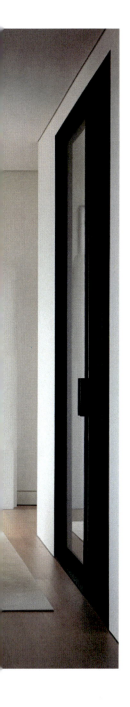

*CONTEM*PORARY

*C*ontemporary interior design is all about reflecting the present moment with a focus on simplicity, functionality, and clean lines. Characterized by its use of neutral color palettes, open spaces, and minimalist aesthetics, this style emphasizes the beauty of less-is-more. Contemporary interiors often feature a blend of textures and materials, such as glass, metal, and natural fibers, to create a balanced and sophisticated look.

Key elements of contemporary design include:

STREAMLINED SILHOUETTES
Furniture and decor often boast sleek, geometric forms with smooth surfaces and minimal ornamentation.

NEUTRAL AND BOLD ACCENTS
A neutral color base is commonly used, with bold accent pieces or artwork adding splashes of color and visual interest.

OPEN SPACES
Emphasis on open floor plans and uncluttered spaces fosters a sense of flow and freedom.

NATURAL LIGHT
Large windows and strategic lighting enhance the sense of openness and highlight the clean lines and simple forms.

TEXTURAL CONTRAST
Incorporating varied textures—such as plush rugs, smooth leather, or polished stone—adds depth and warmth to the otherwise minimalistic design.

THE *CONSOLE* TABLE

BEACHY VIBES

Beachy vibes in interior design evoke the relaxed and refreshing essence of coastal living, bringing the serene beauty of the ocean into your space. This style is all about capturing the laid-back charm and natural elements of beach environments, blending light, airy aesthetics with nautical influences to create a tranquil retreat.

Key elements of beachy vibes in interior design include:

LIGHT AND AIRY COLORS:
Embrace a palette of soft blues, sandy beiges, crisp whites, and gentle greys that mimic the colors of the beach and sky, creating a calm and open feel.

NATURAL MATERIALS

Incorporate materials such as driftwood, rattan, jute, and wicker to bring an organic, earthy quality reminiscent of beachside settings.

TEXTURAL VARIET

Use a mix of textures—like linen, cotton, and soft wool—to enhance comfort and create a layered, inviting atmosphere.

NAUTICAL ACCENTS

Add subtle nautical touches with items like striped patterns, seashell decorations, and maritime-inspired artwork to evoke a sense of coastal adventure.

CASUAL ELEGANCE

Opt for relaxed, comfortable furniture with simple, clean lines that offer a blend of practicality and effortless style.

LIVING AREA

Explore the living area as the central hub of your home with this inspiring collection of images. From cozy, intimate nooks to expansive, open-plan spaces, discover a range of styles and layouts that showcase how this versatile room can serve as both a gathering place and a personal retreat. Whether you seek a modern, minimalist aesthetic or a more traditional, comfortable setting, this section offers a wealth of ideas to help you design a living area that is both functional and beautifully inviting.

THE HEART
OF THE HOUSE

The living area is often considered the heart of the home, serving as the central space where family and friends come together to connect and relax. This section highlights how the living room can be both a vibrant hub for social gatherings and a peaceful retreat for quiet moments. Through a curated selection of inspiring images, explore how different designs and layouts can enhance the functionality and warmth of this pivotal space. From cozy, inviting furnishings to dynamic, open-plan arrangements, discover creative ideas for making your living area a true reflection of your home's character and a welcoming environment for all.

THE SOFA
OR LOVESEAT

The sofa is more than just a piece of furniture; it's the cornerstone of comfort and style in any home. Serving as the primary gathering spot for family, friends, and relaxation, it plays a crucial role in defining the living area's functionality and aesthetic. A well-chosen sofa not only enhances the visual appeal of a room but also provides essential comfort and support, making it a key element in creating a welcoming and functional living space. Whether you prefer a sleek modern design or a plush, traditional look, the right sofa sets the tone for your home's ambiance and everyday living.

MODERN STYLE

Modern style in the living room embraces simplicity, clean lines, and a minimalist approach to design. Characterized by its uncluttered aesthetic, this style focuses on creating a space that feels both open and functional.

By focusing on some key principles, modern style creates a sophisticated living room that feels both stylish and functional, reflecting contemporary elegance with a focus on simplicity. These key principles include:

STREAMLINED FURNITURE

Opt for pieces with geometric shapes and smooth surfaces, such as low-profile sofas and sleek coffee tables, to maintain an open and airy feel.

NEUTRAL COLOR PALETTE

Utilize shades of white, grey, and beige as a base, accented by bold, contrasting colors or subtle textures to add visual interest without overwhelming the space.

NATURAL LIGHT

Maximize natural light with large windows and sheer curtains to enhance the sense of openness and brightness.

MINIMALIST DECOR

Choose a few, carefully selected decor items and artwork that complement the overall design, avoiding excess to keep the space serene and uncluttered.

FUNCTIONAL DESIGN

Emphasize practicality with built-in storage solutions and multi-purpose furniture, ensuring the living room remains organized and versatile.

OH, THE
FIREPLACE

The fireplace serves as both a functional and aesthetic centerpiece in the living room, offering warmth and a touch of classic charm. It's often the heart of the room, providing a cozy gathering spot and enhancing the overall ambiance. A well-designed fireplace can elevate the space, whether through a sleek, modern surround or a traditional mantel.

Key aspects of incorporating a fireplace into your living room include:

DESIGN INTEGRATION

Ensure the fireplace design complements the overall style of the room. A modern fireplace may feature clean lines and a minimalist facade, while a traditional one might include intricate molding and a classic mantel.

VISUAL IMPACT

Use the fireplace as a focal point by arranging furniture around it, creating a natural gathering space. Consider adding a statement piece above the mantel, such as artwork or a mirror, to enhance its visual appeal.

FUNCTIONAL CONSIDERATIONS

In addition to its aesthetic value, a fireplace provides essential warmth. Choose a design that aligns with your heating needs, whether it's a traditional wood-burning fireplace, a gas model, or an electric insert.

DECORATIVE ACCENTS

Complement the fireplace with carefully selected decor items, such as stylish firewood holders, elegant screens, or seasonal decorations, to enhance its role as a central feature of the living room.

SHARP *ANGLES*

Incorporating sharp angles into fireplace design brings a striking, contemporary edge to your living room. This geometric approach transforms the traditional fireplace into a bold architectural statement, blending modern aesthetics with functional elegance.

SMOOTH *CURVES*

Incorporating smooth curves into fireplace design adds a touch of elegance and softness to the living room, creating a serene and inviting focal point. This approach contrasts with the more angular styles, bringing a fluid and graceful aesthetic that enhances the overall ambiance.

OUTDOOR *HEAVEN*

Outdoor fireplaces are a captivating addition to any patio, garden, or backyard, providing both functional warmth and a stylish focal point. They transform outdoor spaces into inviting areas for relaxation and entertainment, extending the enjoyment of your home's living areas beyond the indoors.

THE KITCHEN

The kitchen is more than just a place to cook—it's where functionality meets warmth and style. A well-designed kitchen seamlessly blends form and function, creating a space that is as inviting as it is efficient. From sleek countertops to custom cabinetry, every element should reflect both the personality of the homeowner and the needs of the space. Whether you're drawn to minimalist designs, rustic charm, or modern elegance, the kitchen is a canvas for personal expression and practical innovation. It's where meals are prepared, stories are shared, and memories are made.

THE *CULINARY* HUB

The kitchen is often considered the most dynamic space in a home. It's a place that effortlessly combines practicality with aesthetic appeal, where every detail—from the layout to the choice of materials—plays a crucial role in daily life. In modern design, the kitchen is not only a workspace but also a social gathering point, seamlessly transitioning from meal preparation to entertaining.

LAYOUT AND FLOW

When designing a kitchen, flow and functionality are paramount. An open-concept kitchen, for example, creates an inviting atmosphere, encouraging interaction between the cook and guests. The placement of key elements, such as the stove, sink, and refrigerator, follows the principle of the work triangle, maximizing efficiency and movement.

MATERIALS AND FINISHES

Materials set the tone for the kitchen's aesthetic. Sleek, polished surfaces like marble or quartz bring a sense of luxury and modernity, while wood accents or exposed brick lend warmth and texture. Lighting also plays a pivotal role—task lighting brightens work areas, while ambient lighting sets the mood for social occasions.

STORAGE AND ORGANIZATION

A well-organized kitchen is a joy to work in. Custom cabinetry, pull-out shelves, and hidden storage solutions help maintain a clutter-free environment, enhancing both the visual appeal and usability of the space. A thoughtful design makes everyday tasks smoother and keeps the kitchen looking clean and stylish.

THE KITCHEN ISLAND

A kitchen island serves as the perfect blend of form and function, acting as both a visual anchor and a practical workspace. Whether used for meal prep, dining, or socializing, the island is a versatile feature that enhances the kitchen's overall flow and utility.

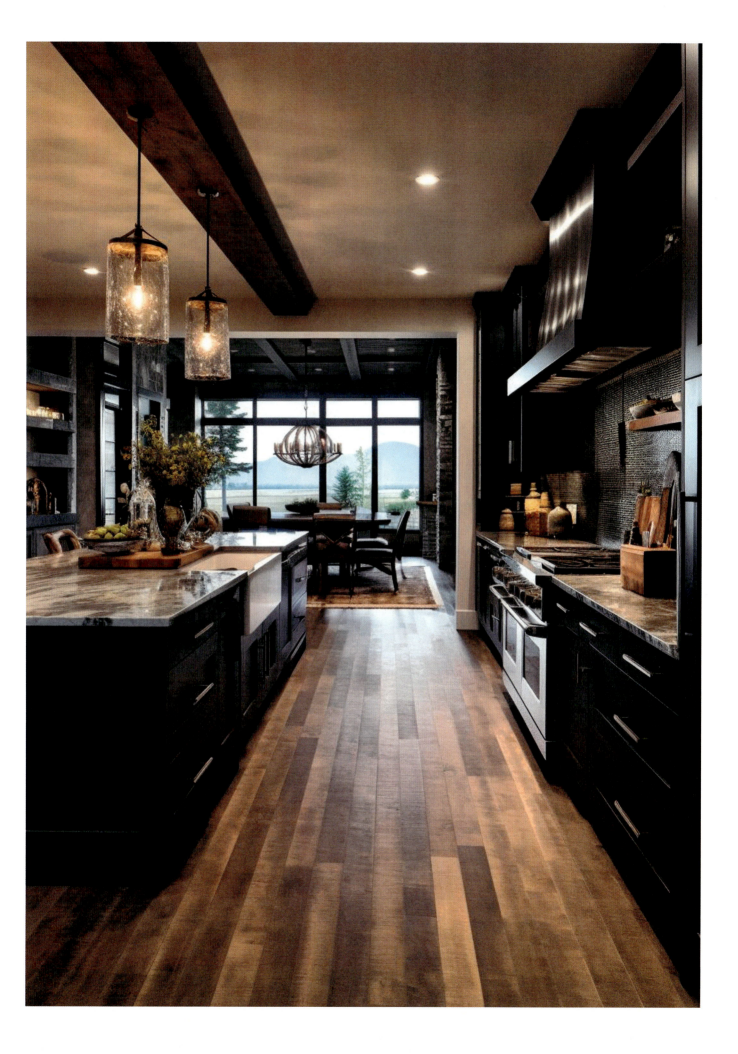

FUNCTIONALITY AT ITS BEST

At its core, the kitchen island provides additional counter space, making it invaluable for food preparation. For larger kitchens, it can house built-in appliances like cooktops, sinks, or wine coolers, transforming the island into a multifunctional hub. Islands with added storage—drawers, cabinets, or open shelving—ensure that everything you need is within easy reach, reducing clutter and improving organization.

A GATHERING SPACE

Beyond its practical uses, the island serves as a social centerpiece. It's where family and friends naturally gravitate, whether for casual meals, morning coffee, or conversation while cooking. Adding bar stools or seating converts the island into an informal dining space, making it ideal for both everyday living and entertaining.

DESIGN AND AESTHETICS

From sleek, modern designs to rustic, farmhouse-inspired styles, kitchen islands can be customized to complement the overall aesthetic of the room. Materials like marble, quartz, or wood can be selected to add texture and elegance. The choice of lighting above the island, such as pendant lights, not only enhances the ambiance but also draws attention to this striking feature.

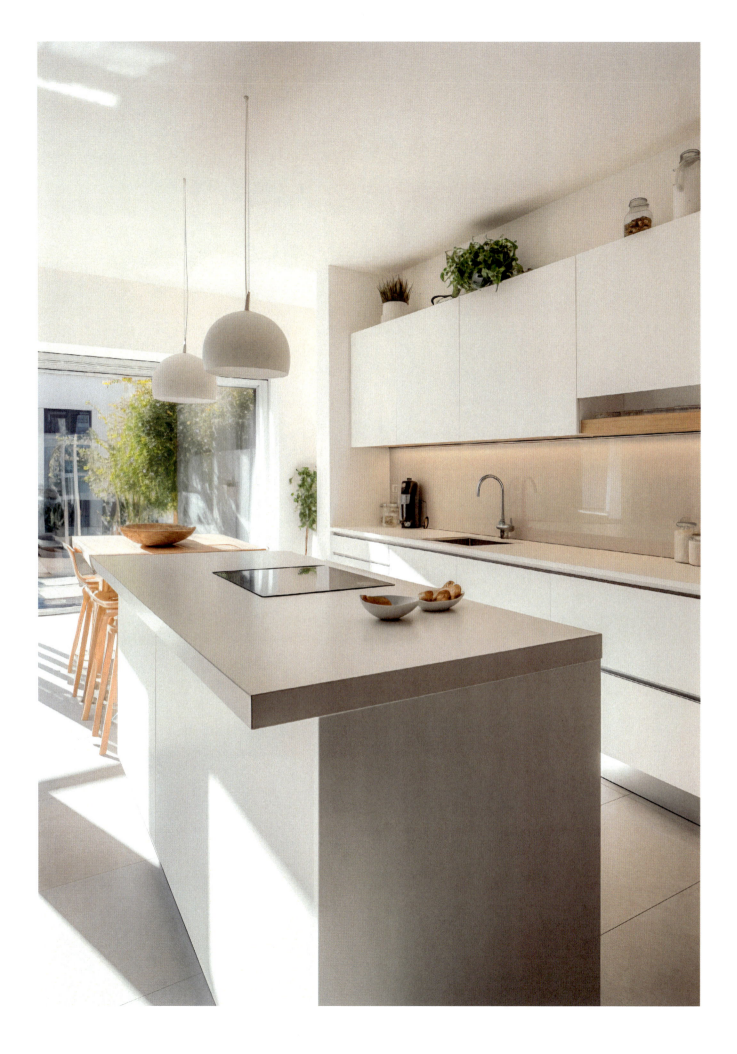

PERSONALIZATION AND CUSTOMIZATION

One of the greatest advantages of a kitchen island is its ability to be tailored to the homeowner's needs. Whether it's adding extra seating, integrating smart technology, or choosing a statement design, the island becomes a highly personalized element that reflects both your lifestyle and design preferences.

from CLASSIC *to* CONTEMPORARY

The style of a kitchen sets the tone for the entire home, reflecting both personal taste and functional needs. Whether you prefer a timeless, traditional design or a sleek, modern aesthetic, the kitchen's style creates an atmosphere that enhances both its usability and visual appeal.

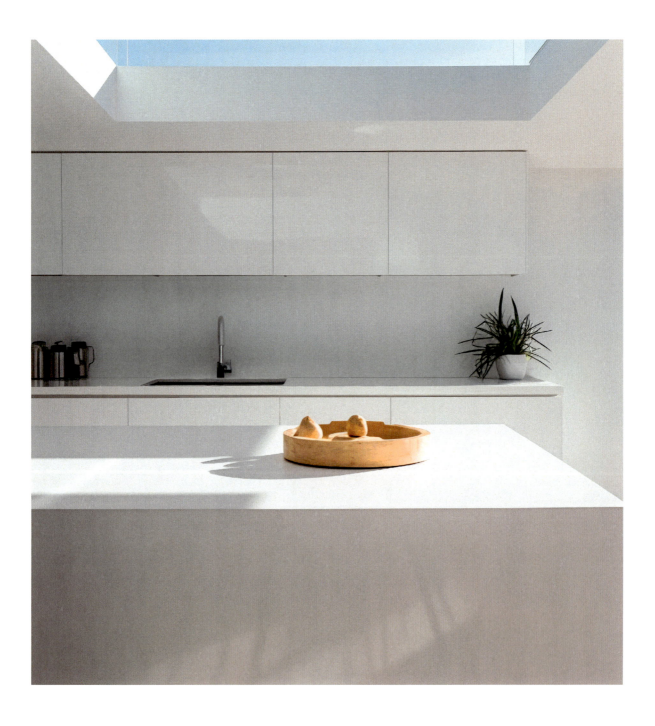

modern KITCHEN

Modern kitchens focus on clean lines, minimalist designs, and efficient use of space. Characterized by sleek materials like stainless steel, quartz, and glass, modern kitchens often feature handleless cabinets, integrated appliances, and neutral color schemes, creating a streamlined look. The emphasis is on functionality and simplicity, making it a popular choice for those who value a clutter-free, contemporary space.

traditional KITCHEN

For a more classic appeal, traditional kitchens embrace rich textures, warm colors, and ornate details. Wood cabinetry, intricate moldings, and natural stone countertops are often key elements in this style. Traditional kitchens may feature elegant finishes such as brass or copper hardware and often incorporate decorative details like raised-panel cabinets or antique-inspired lighting, creating a welcoming and timeless feel.

farmhouse KITCHEN

Farmhouse kitchens are known for their rustic charm and cozy atmosphere. Featuring natural wood, shiplap walls, apron-front sinks, and open shelving, this style blends the old-world warmth of a country kitchen with modern comforts. The use of warm, earthy tones and vintage-inspired fixtures makes farmhouse kitchens inviting and homey, perfect for those who enjoy a lived-in, comfortable space.

THE DINNIG ROOM

The dining room is more than just a place to eat; it's where family and friends gather, conversations flow, and memories are made. Whether it's an intimate dinner or a festive gathering, the design of the dining room plays a pivotal role in creating a welcoming and functional space that enhances every occasion.

A SPACE FOR
CONNECTION
& COMFORT

A well-designed dining room strikes the perfect balance between aesthetics and practicality. The choice of dining table is often the focal point, with its size, shape, and material setting the tone for the room. Round tables encourage conversation, while rectangular tables offer ample space for larger gatherings. The seating, whether upholstered chairs or benches, should be comfortable and complement the overall style of the room.

LIGHTING AS A STATEMENT

Lighting is one of the most important elements in a dining room. A central chandelier or a series of pendant lights not only illuminates the space but also adds a sense of drama and elegance. Dimmer switches allow for flexible lighting options, creating a cozy ambiance for intimate meals and brighter settings for lively events.

MATERIAL CHOICES AND TEXTURE

The materials and textures used in a dining room add depth and warmth. Wood tables and chairs offer a timeless appeal, while glass or marble tables can bring a more modern, refined look. The addition of textiles, such as an area rug, upholstered chairs, or drapery, softens the room and creates a sense of comfort.

PERSONALIZING WITH DÉCOR

Décor plays a key role in personalizing the dining room. From wall art and centerpieces to sideboards and shelving, the right accessories can enhance the room's character. Minimalist settings may feature simple, clean lines, while more eclectic or traditional styles might include detailed table settings, vintage pieces, or family heirlooms.

DESIGN FOR DIFFERENT NEEDS

Dining rooms should be adaptable to different needs and occasions. For homes that entertain frequently, having extendable tables or flexible seating arrangements is essential. In smaller spaces, open-plan designs where the dining area merges with the kitchen or living room can create a seamless flow while maximizing space.

THE DINING TABLE AND CHAIRS

The dining table and chairs are the centerpiece of the dining room, shaping the space both functionally and aesthetically. As the focal point of the room, they set the tone for gatherings and influence the overall atmosphere, making their selection critical to successful design.

THE DINING TABLE

The dining table is not just a surface for meals—it's where daily interactions unfold, from casual breakfasts to formal dinners. Its size, shape, and material impact the room's flow and usability. A round or oval table encourages conversation and is ideal for smaller, more intimate gatherings, while a rectangular or extendable table can accommodate larger groups, making it versatile for entertaining. The material—whether wood, glass, or marble—also affects the room's visual style, with each option contributing a distinct texture and mood. A well-chosen table becomes a foundation for both functionality and style in the dining room.

COMFORTABLE SEATING

Dining chairs must provide comfort and support, as people spend significant time sitting during meals and gatherings. Ergonomically designed chairs with cushioned seats or padded backs ensure comfort for extended periods, while the height and size of the chairs should complement the table to create a balanced, cohesive look. The style of the chairs—whether upholstered, minimalist, or statement pieces—can further enhance the room's design, blending seamlessly with the table or offering a contrasting element for visual interest.

CREATING A
HARMONIOUS BALANCE

The relationship between the table and chairs is key to achieving harmony in the dining room. The proportions must be right: the table should comfortably fit the number of chairs without crowding the space, allowing enough room for movement. The materials, colors, and finishes should either match or complement each other to create a unified design. For instance, a sleek, modern table pairs well with minimalist chairs, while a rustic wooden table might be complemented by more traditional, upholstered seating.

THE BATH *ROOM*

The modern bathroom is no longer just a utilitarian space; it has evolved into a personal sanctuary that blends functionality with luxury and design. As one of the most intimate areas in the home, the bathroom serves multiple purposes, from daily routines to moments of relaxation, and its design must reflect both practicality and aesthetic appeal.

DESIGN FOR DIFFERENT NEEDS

A well-designed bathroom maximizes space and promotes efficiency without sacrificing comfort. The layout should allow for smooth movement between key elements like the sink, shower, and toilet. Compact spaces benefit from clever storage solutions such as floating vanities, recessed shelving, or built-in niches in showers, which help keep the room clutter-free and visually open. Ergonomic considerations are also essential, ensuring that fixtures are positioned at comfortable heights and that there's ample space for ease of use.

MATERIAL SELECTION: DURABILITY MEETS ELEGANCE

Bathrooms are subject to high levels of moisture and humidity, making material selection critical. Porcelain, ceramic, and natural stone are popular choices for flooring and walls due to their durability and water resistance. These materials also offer an array of textures and finishes that can enhance the bathroom's aesthetic. For a more luxurious touch, incorporating marble countertops, mosaic tiles, or custom cabinetry can elevate the space. Using high-quality materials ensures longevity while also contributing to the overall design language of the bathroom.

LIGHTING & AMBIANCE

Proper lighting plays a vital role in the bathroom's functionality and mood. Layered lighting—combining ambient, task, and accent lighting—ensures that the space is both well-lit and adaptable to different activities. Task lighting around mirrors is crucial for grooming, while softer, dimmable lighting can create a relaxing atmosphere for baths. The inclusion of natural light through windows or skylights adds warmth and open-ness, enhancing the room's sense of serenity.

DESIGN
EXPRESSION

While functionality is paramount, the bathroom also offers an opportunity for creative expression. From bold tile patterns and unique vanities to statement mirrors and artwork, every detail can reflect the personality of the homeowner. Whether it's a sleek, minimalist design or a more ornate, classic style, personalization adds character and makes the space truly your own.

DOUBLE OR NOTHING

A double vanity is a popular feature in modern bathroom design, offering both practical benefits and aesthetic appeal. With two sinks, ample countertop space, and additional storage, a double vanity enhances the functionality of a bathroom, making it especially ideal for shared spaces.

FIXTURES & FINISHES

Bathroom fixtures, from faucets to showerheads, are not only practical elements but also key design statements. Sleek chrome or brushed brass fixtures can create a modern, sophisticated look, while oil-rubbed bronze or matte black finishes introduce an industrial or vintage flair. The choice of fixtures should align with the overall design theme, whether minimalist, classic, or eclectic, and provide both style and functionality.

WELLNESS &
SPA-LIKE FEATURES

As bathrooms increasingly become spaces for relaxation, many designs incorporate spa-like features. Freestanding tubs, rainfall showers, heated floors, and steam rooms can transform a simple bathroom into a luxurious retreat. The growing trend of wellness-focused designs emphasizes the importance of creating an environment that nurtures both body and mind, where the bathroom becomes a space for rejuvenation and self-care.

THE LAUNDRY *ROOM*

Often overlooked, the laundry room plays an essential role in the home, offering a dedicated space for cleaning, organization, and storage. Thoughtful design transforms this utilitarian area into a highly functional and efficient space that not only makes laundry tasks easier but also enhances the overall flow of the home.

OPTIMIZING
LAYOUT & FLOW

A well-planned layout is key to the success of any laundry room. Whether in a compact space or a larger, dedicated area, the flow should allow for ease of movement between tasks like washing, drying, folding, and storing. Ideally, the washer and dryer are placed side by side or stacked to maximize space, while countertops or folding stations provide ample surface area for sorting and folding clothes. Efficient layouts keep everything within reach, minimizing the effort required for everyday chores.

STORAGE
SOLUTIONS

Smart storage is crucial in a laundry room to maintain a clean and organized environment. Custom cabinetry, built-in shelves, and pull-out hampers help store detergents, cleaning supplies, and laundry baskets while keeping clutter out of sight. Overhead cabinets or open shelving can provide additional space for storing extra linens or seasonal items, ensuring that the laundry room remains functional yet organized.

STORAGE SOLUTIONS

Smart storage is crucial in a laundry room to maintain a clean and organized environment. Custom cabinetry, built-in shelves, and pull-out hampers help store detergents, cleaning supplies, and laundry baskets while keeping clutter out of sight. Overhead cabinets or open shelving can provide additional space for storing extra linens or seasonal items, ensuring that the laundry room remains functional yet organized.

THE MAIN
BEDROOM

The bedroom is often considered the most personal and restful space in a home, a retreat designed for relaxation and rejuvenation. Its design typically prioritizes comfort, function, and personal expression, making it one of the most customizable rooms in a home.

LAYOUT AND FUNCTIONALITY

When designing a bedroom, the layout should be intuitive and facilitate easy movement. Positioning the bed as the focal point, typically against a solid wall, helps establish a sense of grounding and balance. Clear paths to closets, windows, and other functional areas are important to avoid clutter and create a calming atmosphere.

THE BED

The bed is the centerpiece of any bedroom. Its size, style, and placement are crucial. A bed frame should complement the overall aesthetic, whether it's minimalist, rustic, or opulent. High-quality bedding—layered with soft sheets, plush pillows, and comforting duvets—enhances the sense of luxury and coziness.

LIGHTING

Thoughtful lighting transforms a bedroom from just a sleeping space to a soothing environment. Natural light is ideal for daytime use, with sheer curtains allowing light to filter in softly. At night, ambient lighting from bedside lamps, dimmable overhead fixtures, or even strategically placed LED strips can set a tranquil mood. Task lighting near reading areas or vanities ensures practicality without overpowering the space

COLOR & *MATERIALS*

Calming, neutral tones such as soft whites, grays, or pastels are often favored for bedroom walls, promoting a peaceful atmosphere conducive to rest. However, bold accents—whether through artwork, bedding, or accent walls—can bring personality to the room. Natural materials, such as wood, linen, or wool, also contribute to a serene and grounding environment.

TEXTILES & BEDDING

The selection of textiles in a bedroom contributes to both its visual warmth and physical comfort. Layering different fabrics—such as cotton sheets, wool throws, and velvet pillows—not only adds texture but also serves functional purposes throughout the seasons. High-quality bedding can make all the difference in creating a restful environment. In colder months, layers of blankets and plush pillows enhance warmth, while in the summer, breathable linens keep the space cool and inviting.

COLOR PALETTE AND MOOD

Color plays a central role in influencing mood, especially in a space meant for relaxation. Soft, neutral tones such as grays, creams, and pastels tend to promote calmness, making them ideal for bedrooms. However, deeper hues like navy, emerald green, or charcoal can add depth and richness, transforming the room into a more intimate, cocoon-like retreat.

PERSONAL
TOUCHES

Finally, the bedroom is a deeply personal space, so it should reflect the tastes and personality of its inhabitant. Family photos, artwork, or meaningful objects can help make the room feel like a sanctuary.

KIDS BEDROOM
& NURSERY

A kid's bedroom is more than just a place to sleep—it's a multi-functional space for playing, learning, and growing. As children's needs evolve quickly, the design of their bedroom should be adaptable while also fostering creativity and comfort.

SPACE FOR
IMAGINATION
& PLAY

For younger children, their bedroom often serves as a creative playground. It's essential to create a space where they feel free to imagine, explore, and play. Open floor areas for activities like building with blocks, playing with toys, or even having a mini performance stage should be incorporated into the design. Storage solutions like cubbies or baskets keep the room organized while making it easy for children to access their toys and games.

THEMES

Themes can also play a huge role in sparking imagination. Whether the theme is based on a favorite animal, outer space, or a sports hobby, incorporating themed elements like bedding, wall art, or even wallpaper can create a magical, personalized environment. However, keep in mind that kids' interests change quickly, so designing a flexible base allows for easy updates.

FUNCTIONAL STORAGE SOLUTIONS

As kids grow, so do their belongings. From clothes and toys to books and art supplies, having effective storage is essential for keeping a kid's room organized. Choose multi-functional furniture, such as beds with storage underneath, bookcases that double as toy displays, or dressers that can hold both clothes and art materials.

CREATING COZY
SLEEPING SPACES

The bed is central to a kid's room, both functionally and as a design element. Bunk beds or lofted beds can maximize vertical space, which is great for smaller rooms, freeing up floor space for activities. Fun, colorful bedding can make the sleeping area inviting and exciting, while ensuring comfort and safety is always a priority. Beds with built-in drawers can also provide extra storage, essential for keeping clutter at bay. For very young children, consider adding elements like soft rugs or cushions on the floor to create a cozy reading nook or relaxation space where they can unwind before bed.

STUDY & LEARNING ZONES

As children reach school age, incorporating a dedicated study area becomes important. A small desk with an adjustable chair and good lighting creates a designated space for homework, crafts, and other learning activities. The desk setup should be both ergonomic and creative, encouraging focus while also serving as an inspirational space for artistic expression. Personalized touches, such as a corkboard for displaying art or assignments, can make the area feel unique to the child.

DESIGNING A
NURSERY ROOM

A nursery is a special space designed to nurture and comfort both baby and parents. It's a room that balances beauty, functionality, and tranquility, as the right design can help promote restful sleep for the baby and ease of use for caregivers. When setting up a nursery, thoughtful consideration goes into every element—from furniture to colors and lighting—creating an environment that is soothing and practical. The primary purpose of a nursery is to serve as a peaceful place where babies can sleep and be cared for. The layout should prioritize ease of use, especially for parents who will be spending significant time in the room for feeding, changing, and putting the baby to sleep.

REST &
PRACTICALITY

Color plays a significant role in the overall ambiance of the nursery. Soft, neutral tones like pale grays, whites, creams, or pastels create a soothing environment that promotes relaxation and sleep. Avoid overly bright or stimulating colors like bold reds or oranges, which can be energizing instead of calming. Accents in gentle tones—soft pinks, blues, or yellows—can add warmth and personality without overwhelming the room. Nursery lighting should be soft and gentle to create a cozy atmosphere that encourages sleep. Overhead lighting can be harsh, so consider using dimmable lights or soft, indirect lamps.